Small Apartments

Editor: **Paco Asensio**

Editorial coordination and texts: **Alejandro Bahamón**

Translation: **Wendy Griswold**

Art direction: **Mireia Casanovas Soley**

Graphic design and layout: **Pilar Cano**

First published in 2003 by Harper Design International,
an imprint of HarperCollins Publishers
10 East 53rd Street, New York, NY 10022-5299

Distributed throughout the world
by HarperCollins International
10 East 53rd Street, New York, NY 10022-5299
Fax: 212-207-7654

Editorial project:

2003 © **LOFT** Publications
Domènech 7-9, 2º 2ª. 08012 Barcelona, Spain
Tel.: +34 932 183 099
Fax: +34 932 370 060
loft@loftpublications.com
www.loftpublications.com

Hardcover ISBN: 0-06-008768-4
Paperback ISBN: 0-06-054634-4
D.L.: B-37.872-02

Printed by: Gràfiques Anman del Vallès. Barberà del Vallès. Spain

If you would like to suggest projects for inclusion in our next
volumes, please e-mail details to us at: **loft@loftpublications.com**

Small Apartments

HARPER
DESIGN
international

CONTENTS

FUNCTIONAL FURNISHINGS

Over the past several decades, the city has evolved into a place in which the home, largely as a result of the commercialization and deterioration of public space, takes on greater character and personality. The density of large cities and the desire for an individualized home have created a style of space to which we have now become quite accustomed. This is the small apartment which, as the tiniest of homes, reflects a lifestyle characteristic of our times. These residences are true interior landscapes, linked to other compact elements of contemporary life – the laptop, the mobile phone, light meals, or the most sophisticated audio/video systems – that tend to save time, motion, and usable space in the modern home. These technologies, applied to the design of small living spaces, best represent life in the big city today.

Technological advances and changes in many of our daily routines do not necessarily translate into substantial changes in the inner workings of a small apartment as compared to a conventional home. The plan stays pretty much the same, with even a tiny apartment having some extra touches, such as studies or reading niches. The major difference lies in the strategies that architects and designers use to take full advantage of the space and emphasize the architectural features of each home. These

COLOR

MOVABLE PANELS

become fundamental tools for understanding how architects, designers, or owners of small apartments approach a project involving minimal living space.

Many interior design strategies are common to all the apartments. We see multiple instances in which a combination of functions is carried out in the same space, traffic areas are minimized, non-structural interior partitions are eliminated, and light, transparent materials are employed. But there are also very different ways of designing a small home, from the spontaneity of an appropriated décor to the purest design ideas that go into the smallest detail of the architectural project. While all the examples employ different solutions, combining various design strategies to use the space

apartments stand out precisely because of the ingenious way in which housing needs have been adapted to minimal space without sacrificing quality or comfort.

This compilation of projects from around the world pays special attention to the particular features of each space. While none of the apartments exceeds 800 square feet, all are homes, and the design strategies are very similar – in each case, the end result is determined by the pre-existing features. The property's location within the city, the building's architectural characteristics, its structure, and the lighting and ventilation conditions are points of departure for the interior design. They

to its best advantage, each is organized around five aspects that are considered essential to solving interior design problems and that become the most important features of each apartment: functional furnishings, color, movable panels, restraint, and the exterior. This, however, does not mean that other important aspects are ignored or that the smallest details are not in keeping with the basic concept.

RESTRAINT

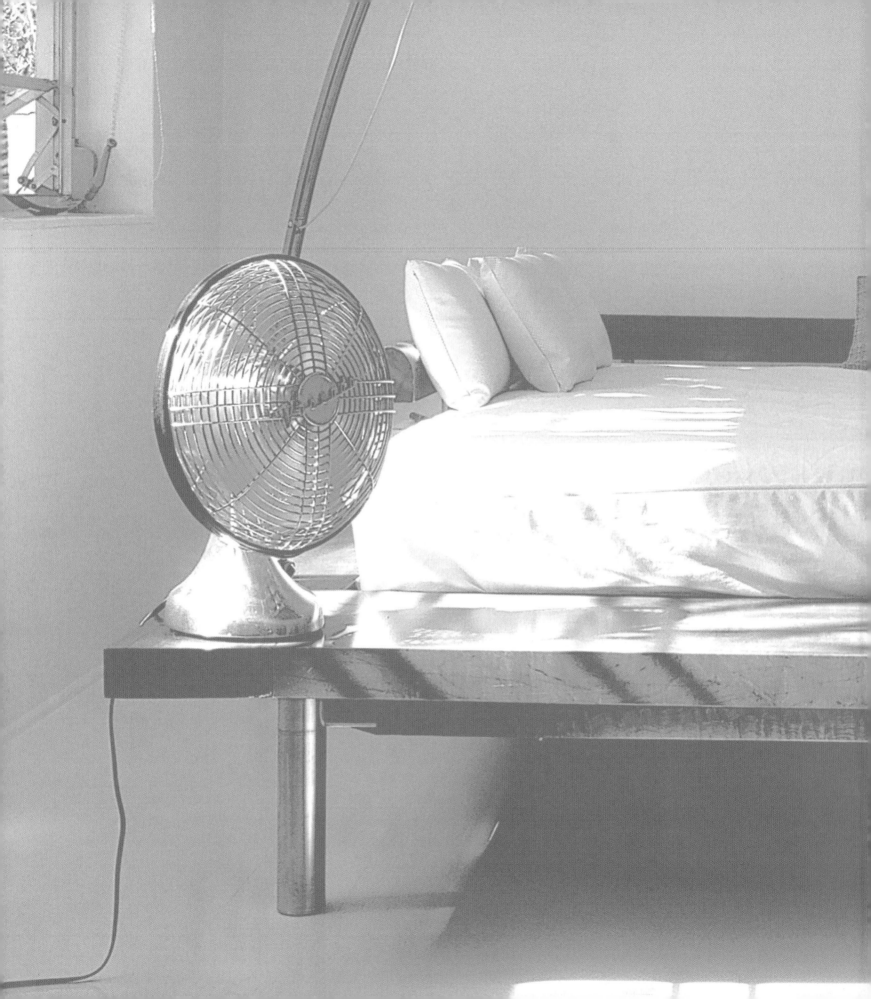

FUNCTIONAL FURNISHINGS

The furnishings in a small apartment are generally chosen on the basis of their ability to fulfill multiple functions and fit the space to the centimeter. Rarely do we find showy, non-functional, or antique furniture or stand-alone storage space. On the contrary, the furnishings are generally custom designed, using every inch of space efficiently and supporting various household functions. Units that serve as bookshelves and as kitchen fixtures, closets that house a lavatory, and fold-away desks are some of the features that do double duty and are totally integrated with the existing elements.

Apartment on Flinders Lane

ARCHITECT: **STAUGHTON ARCHITECTS** LOCATION: **MELBOURNE, AUSTRALIA** AREA: **850 SQ. FEET** DATE: **2000**
PHOTOGRAPHY: **SHANNON MCGRATH**

This space is located in an old office building in the heart of Melbourne, Australia that was converted to an apartment complex. Since the building is elongated and on a corner, the apartments have windows facing the exterior, and vertical traffic is confined to the two ends. Although the exterior still looks the same as it did when the building was new – even the original windows were retained – the interior is surprising because of its contemporary design and warm atmosphere, reflecting the lifestyle in this district, which is undergoing an urban renewal process.

The project is defined by two principal elements. The first is a multifunctional, free-standing wood-framed unit that encloses the sleeping area, provides storage space, serves as an auxiliary dining room, includes bookshelves, and is a sculptural element in and of itself. This unit is self-supporting, touching neither the ceiling nor the lateral walls, and looks almost like a piece of furniture. The second element is the set of patterns sandblasted into the original cement floor. These patterns, with their polished texture, are reminiscent of the diagrams used by the architects in their design plans and contrast with the previous floor covering.

The layout is very simple. The wood and polycarbonate unit dynamically divides the space. On the one hand, it separates the space into two clearly defined areas: bedroom and living room. On the other hand, it delimits the kitchen and guides traffic to the narrow entrance of the bedroom and the bathroom. The space where the patterns on the floor simply suggest ways to approach the layout and accommodate the furnishings was left completely open.

STAUGHTON ARCHITECTS

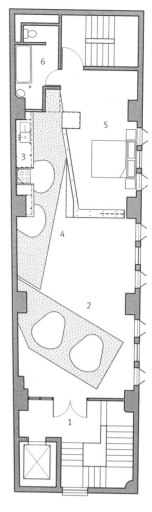

Plan

1. Entrance
2. Living room
3. Kitchen
4. Dining room
5. Bedroom
6. Bathroom

The industrial character of the space was maintained by retaining elements such as the original ventilation ducts, wrought iron, piping, and the original flooring.

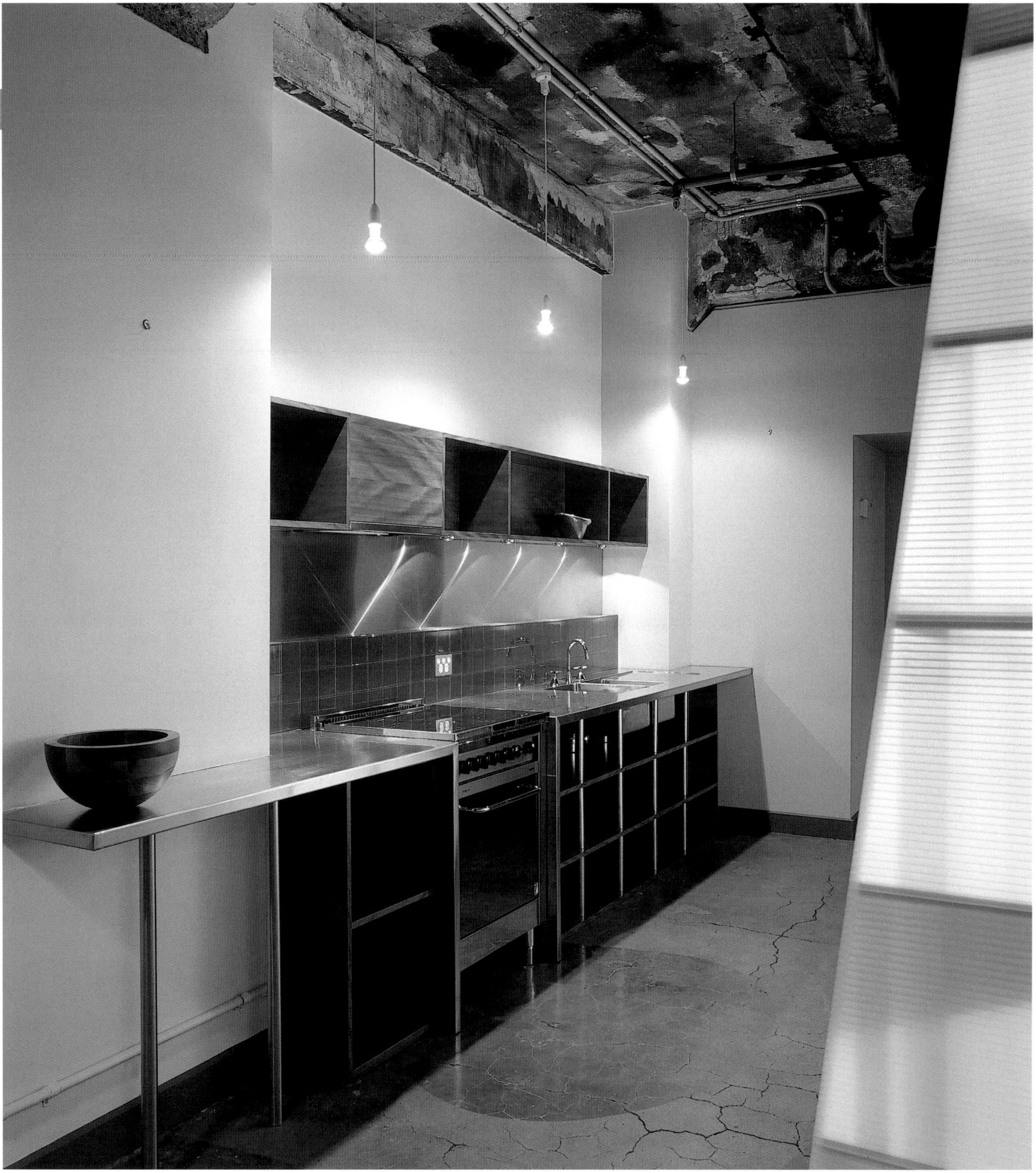

In addition to performing multiple functions, the polycarbonate and wood unit also acts as a lamp, behind which shadows are visible.

La Magdalena Apartment

ARCHITECT: **Guillermo Arias** LOCATION: **Bogota, Colombia** AREA: **665 sq. feet** DATE: **1996**
PHOTOGRAPHY: **Pablo Rojas + Álvaro Gutiérrez**

Although a much larger apartment was subdivided to create this one, the best features of the original structure were preserved. It is located in downtown Bogota, in a 1930s building which still has the principal façade, glorious views of a quiet, tree-lined street, and original features, such as the stone fireplace. The renovation project tried to create an efficient home while retaining the intrinsic al character of the space.

The plan called for a fully-integrated space, with the living room and bedroom located in what was originally the salon. A white-painted wooden unit unobtrusively divides these two areas and does duty as a bookcase, television cabinet, and music center. This piece was placed away from the side walls rather than up against them to avoid breaking the continuity of the space. On one side of the fireplace is the kitchen, which appears to be a continuation of the living room; and on the other side of the fireplace are the dressing room and bathroom, next to the entrance. A mirrored door that also contains storage space ensures total privacy for the lavatory, which is the only area that can be completely closed off.

The color white dominates the entire apartment — even the furniture and the original wood floor are white. This achieves a sensation of spaciousness and abundant light. In contrast, the kitchen walls were painted with red enamel, the baseboard and countertop are black granite, and the furnishings are natural wood. Here, most of the elements were left open to view to take advantage of every inch of space. Many details, such as the molding for the false ceiling and the lamps, were designed by the architect himself to preserve the original character of the space to the greatest possible extent.

Guillermo Arias

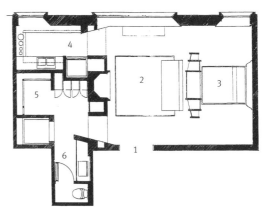

PLAN

IN THE LIVING AREAS, BEDROOM, AND BATH, THE DOMINANT COLOR IS WHITE. MANY OF THE ACCENT PIECES WERE DESIGNED WITH THE ORIGINAL CHARACTER OF THE SPACE IN MIND.

1. ENTRANCE
2. LIVING ROOM
3. BEDROOM
4. KITCHEN
5. CLOSET
6. BATHROOM

THE KITCHEN FURNISHINGS TAKE FULL ADVANTAGE OF EVERY INCH OF SPACE, LEAVING
MOST OF THE ELEMENTS OPEN TO VIEW. THIS CREATES A PLAY OF TEXTURES
AND COLORS THAT CONTRAST WITH THE REST OF THE APARTMENT.

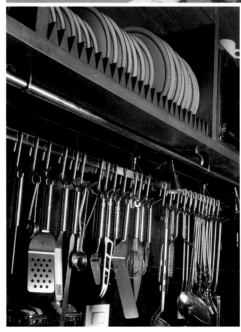

WEST VILLAGE APARTMENT

ARCHITECTS: **DESAI / CHIA STUDIO** LOCATION: **NEW YORK CITY, UNITED STATES** AREA: **645 SQ. FEET** DATE: **2000**
PHOTOGRAPHY: **JOSHUA McHUGH**

The owners of this apartment live for the most part in New Mexico, but needed a small place in New York where they could stay while enjoying the city's cultural activities. The design had to be flexible enough to permit entertaining and to accommodate visitors for short periods in a minimal space.

After removing the partitions that divided the interior, the designers concentrated all activities in a central space. Grouping the service areas, such as the kitchen, bathroom, and laundry room, on a side wall ensured efficient use of the space while optimizing placement of the fixtures.

A small sleeping loft above the kitchen was built with slender lengths of stainless steel to leave as much space as possible both above and below the platform. In addition to creating a small extra bedroom, it acts as a backdrop for the living area. Lights built into the loft's frame illuminate the kitchen as well as the sleeping area, while the wooden planks add a touch of warmth to both. This level is reached by a slender, riserless stainless steel stairway that lets the users see beyond the stairs into the space below the loft.

A storage unit made of lacquered panels is the only element separating the bedroom from the rest of the apartment. It houses the sound system and television; since it does not reach the ceiling, it emphasizes the continuity of the space. The bathroom is finished in polished cement and stucco, while the kitchen counter is a single cement slab. A frosted glass door allows natural light to flow into the bathroom while also shedding light into the foyer.

DESAI / CHIA STUDIO

THE HEIGHT OF THE SPACE WAS TAKEN ADVANTAGE OF AND A SLEEPING PLATFORM WAS PLACED ABOVE THE KITCHEN. IN ADDITION TO CREATING ADDITIONAL SPACE, THIS PRODUCED AN INTERESTING VISUAL ELEMENT, ADDING SCALE AND DEPTH TO THE KITCHEN.

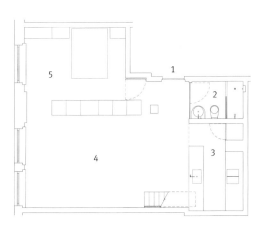

PLAN

1. ENTRANCE
2. BATHROOM
3. KITCHEN
4. LIVING ROOM/DINING ROOM
5. BEDROOM

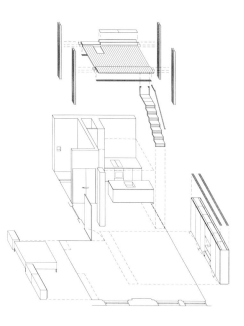

AXONOMETRIC WIEW

THE UNIT THAT HOUSES THE TELEVISION ALSO
SEPARATES THE CENTRAL AREA FROM THE BEDROOM.
IN THE BATHROOM, THE SIMPLE LINES ARE STRIKING
AND THE GLASS DOOR LETS LIGHT SHINE IN.

Apartment on Michigan Avenue

Architect: Pablo Uribe **Collaborator: Guillermo Arias (design of bed and lighting design)**
Location: Miami, United States **Area: 430 sq. feet** **Date: 2000** **Photography: Pep Escoda**

This efficient, square-shaped apartment is on the second floor of a 1951 building in the heart of Miami Beach. Despite its small size, it retains the architectural character of the era. The view of the interior garden it shares with the rest of the complex adds to the feeling of spaciousness.

Each of the four principal units into which the apartment is divided – the living room/ bedroom/dining room, the study/kitchen, the corridor, and the bathroom – has its own set of functions. The living room/bedroom/dining room and the study/kitchen are connected by a wide area which accentuates the fluidity of the space even more. But the bathroom is only accessible by a corridor, so it is totally separated from the principal space. The overall effect is of clean lines and elegance.

Several architectural elements, such as the aluminum windows, were restored to enhance the 1950s feel. The bathroom layout and the kitchen furnishings remained intact. The original wood floor was painted white to create a contemporary atmosphere while enhancing the feeling of spaciousness and playing with the "endless" effect used in photography studios.

The furniture was chosen to make the best use of the limited space, creating a series of multifunctional areas, hence the idea of an opium bed as a central feature. By day a large sofa and point of visual focus, it becomes the bed at night. Functions were added to those normally ascribed to the kitchen and living room, including a reading niche placed in the kitchen and the dining area incorporated as part of the living room. Finally, the 22 feet long towel rack in the corridor plays an important role, making the hall a place where towels and swimsuits are hung to dry, indelibly imprinting the "beach" theme which is so much a part of this city.

Pablo Uribe

THE LARGE BED-SOFA DOMINATES THE SPACE. SITUATED IN THE CENTER OF THE
APARTMENT IN AN AREA WITH FEW OTHER ELEMENTS TO DETRACT ATTENTION FROM IT
OR ADD CLUTTER, IT CREATES A SETTING IN WHICH VARIOUS ACTIVITIES ARE CARRIED OUT.

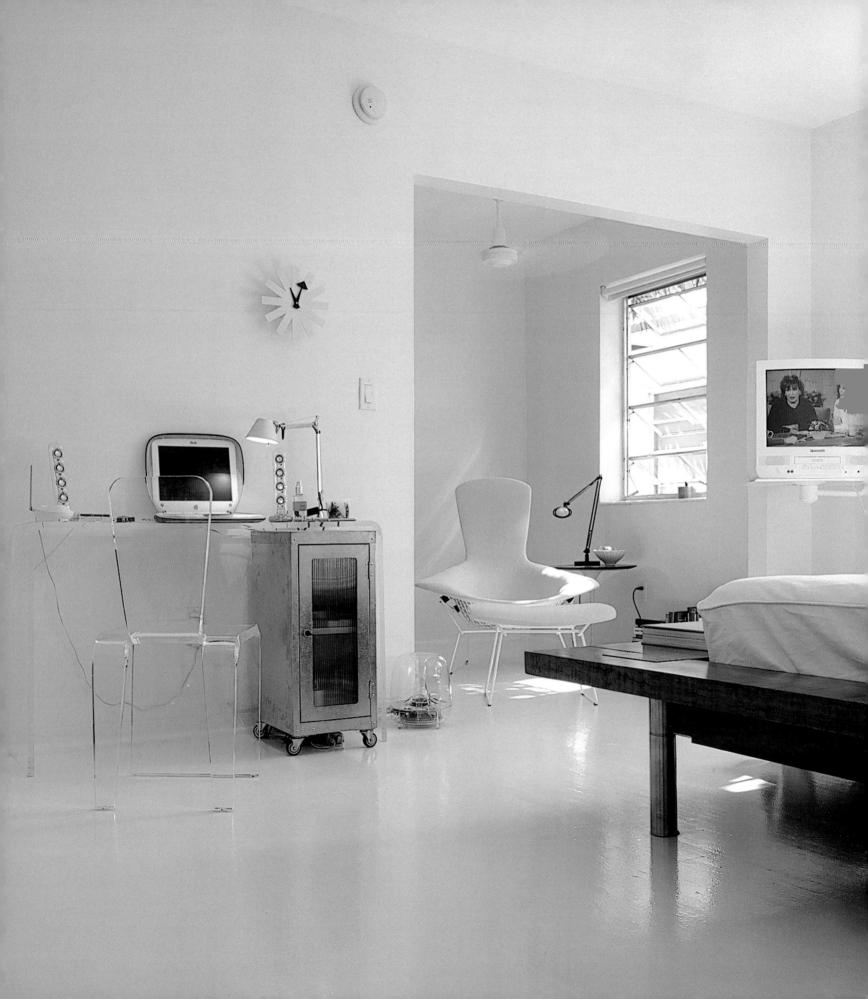

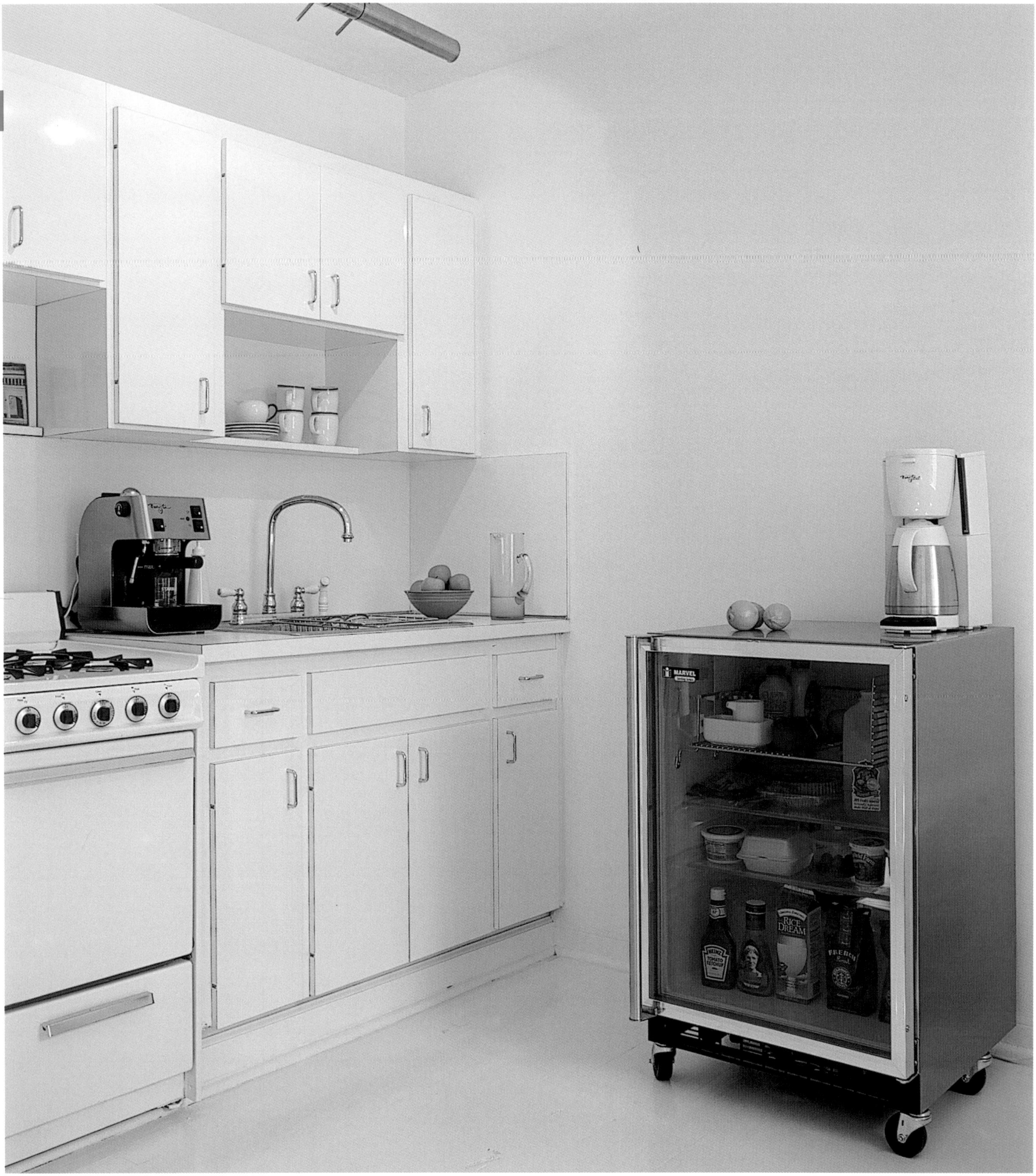
MARVEL
RICE DREAM

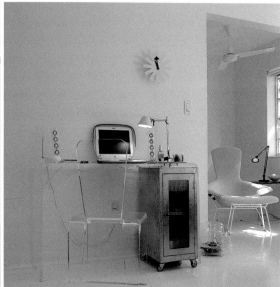

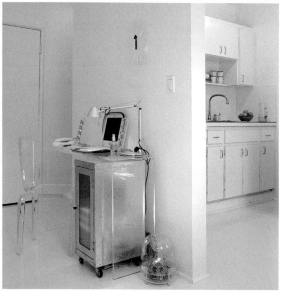

EVERY PIECE OF FURNITURE, WHETHER SPECIALLY DESIGNED OR FOUND IN STORES AND MARKETS, ENHANCES THE ORIGINAL CHARACTER OF THE SPACE.

Bishop's Mansions Apartment

ARCHITECT: **Pablo Uribe** LOCATION: **London, United Kingdom** AREA: **806 sq. feet** DATE: **2000**
PHOTOGRAPHY: **Montse Garriga**

This apartment's exceptional location, on the ground floor of a house in Fulham, London that dates back to 1900, makes for an especially peaceful setting. The front yard, where the entrance is located, and the rear garden, which is shared with the rest of the neighborhood, provide all the rooms with natural light while the trees and shrubs grant a sense of tranquility.

Renovation dramatically changed the interior configuration, taking best achieving a feeling of spaciousness. As in the majority of Victorian houses, the space had been divided into rooms off a long corridor. The architect eliminated all the non-structural walls and created a series of areas, from the front yard to the rear garden, where household activities can take place in a single setting.

The home's new configuration eliminated a second bedroom and used the space for the social area and the new bathroom, done in silver, where the bathtub was sacrificed in favor of a large new shower. To maintain an unobstructed traffic pattern, the master bedroom was connected with the rest of the apartment by a unique unit that serves two purposes: on one side, it is a wall and support for the bed, and on the other side it's an armoire which marks off the space used as a dressing room.

The architect drew his inspiration from the work of Adolf Loos, whose settings are known for their great warmth and visual richness, well suited to the London climate.

Cherry wood was chosen for the cabinets and the wall paneling, and mahogany was used for the piece that separates the bed from the dressing room. In the kitchen, all the appliances are hidden behind cherry wood doors, so the kitchen is fully integrated with the living and dining areas.

Pablo Uribe

A COLLAPSIBLE TABLE MAKES IT POSSIBLE TO USE
THE SPACE NEXT TO THE KITCHEN AS A DINING AREA
OR AS ANOTHER SMALL LIVING ROOM INTEGRATED
WITH THE REST OF THE APARTMENT.

Although the renovation completely breaks with the original Victorian style, it employs materials that connect with that type of architecture. The unfinished brick, dark wood, and light colors help create a warm, inviting atmosphere.

Apartment on Rue Rochechouart

Architect: **Peter Tyberghien** Interior designer: **Bruno Pascal** Location: **Paris, France** Area: **333 sq. feet**
Date: **2000** Photography: **Alejandro Bahamón**

More than an apartment, this is a spacious, luxurious home with every comfort for short stays in central Paris. The clients commissioned this project because several years earlier they had tried to find a romantic but contemporary hotel where they could celebrate their tenth wedding anniversary. Unable to find the type of place they were looking for, they decided to create it themselves. The building's prime location and the apartment's excellent lighting convinced them that this was the place.

Despite its small size, the apartment was originally divided into a bedroom, kitchen, bathroom, and living room. The first step in the renovation was to tear down all the interior walls dividing the space and, taking advantage of the absence of structural elements, create a single, open space. The slightly longitudinal proportions and the presence of two windows on the main façade were the jumping off points for the creation of the new layout. Against the wall opposite the windows, where the entrance is located, are all the service areas. A series of folding doors hide the tiny kitchen, which can be integrated into the space, the closet, and the bathroom, the only independent element.

A liquid crystal partition whose appearance can change from transparent to frosted at the touch of a button separates the bed from the bathtub. A large, flat, space-saving screen is complemented by professional music and video equipment.

The finishes and furnishings are replete with details that define the project and make this apartment a sophisticated, comfortable, relaxing place.

Peter Tyberghien

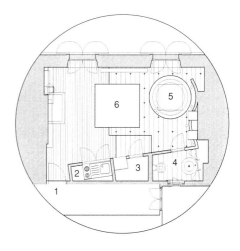

PLAN

1. ENTRANCE
2. KITCHEN
3. CLOSET
4. BATHROOM
5. BATH
6. BED

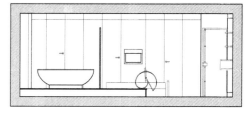

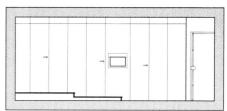

SECTIONS

BUILT INTO THE SAME SERVICE UNIT, NEXT TO THE CUPBOARD-LIKE STRUCTURE THAT CONTAINS THE KITCHEN, IS A PROFESSIONAL COFFEE MAKER THAT GRINDS BEANS FOR IMMEDIATE USE. THE STAINLESS STEEL DETAILS SERVE AS SUPPORT FOR THE LIGHTING AND AS SMALL SHELVES.

THANKS TO THE UNIQUE LAYOUT, THE VIDEO SYSTEM CAN BE ENJOYED FROM THE BATHTUB. THE WALL CONTAINING THE WINDOWS WAS PAINTED DARK GRAY FOR GREATER CONTRAST AND DRAMA.

COLOR

The cliché that white is the only solution for small spaces is totally disproved by the way color is used in the following apartments. The use of varying tones in the same space can help differentiate the activities carried out while creating a highly diverse interior landscape. A color can also help unify the elements of a home, add warmth and brightness to a setting rendered lifeless by the lighting conditions, or highlight certain design elements. In any event, the appropriate use of color is the most effective way to add character to a space without resorting to sophisticated or costly techniques.

APARTMENT ON BARÓ DE LA BARRE

ARCHITECTS: **ARACELI MANZANO, Mª JOSÉ MANZANO, ESTHER FLAVIA** LOCATION: **BARCELONA, SPAIN**
AREA: **540 SQ. FEET** DATE: **1999** PHOTOGRAPHY: **EUGENI PONS**

The renovation of this 540 square-foot space into comfortable, pleasant rooms presented quite a challenge. Located in Barcelona's Zona Alta, near the mountain, this apartment has just one large opening to the exterior. This was a determining factor of the interior configuration.

Minimizing the interior divisions was the first step toward opening up the space visually while using the large window for light and ventilation. The living room, dining room, kitchen, and bedroom share a single space, while the bathroom and dressing room are the only areas that are totally closed off. The furniture is arranged to define and close off the bathroom while affording storage space in both the bathroom and living room.

Warm, cozy spaces were created by taking advantage of the abundant natural light. Highly functional furniture with simple lines ensures efficient use of the space. The area in which daytime activities take place is near the window, while the space farthest from it is reserved for sleeping. The kitchen furniture and the cabinets housing the washing machine were designed especially for this project and make it easy to access all the appliances.

The details of the furnishings define the space and highlight the function of every corner of the home. Long shelves, multi-purpose storage units, and drawers under the bed are some of the touches that help make this apartment a flexible, comfortable place. Thanks to the neutral tone of the merbau wood flooring, striking colors can be used in the rest of the space. The sleeping area is defined by a platform of varnished wood chipboard which can also be used as a large storage compartment.

ARACELI MANZANO
Mª JOSÉ MANZANO
ESTHER FLAVIA

PLAN

1. ENTRANCE
2. STUDIO
3. BED
4. CLOSET
5. DINING ROOM
6. LIVING ROOM
7. KITCHEN
8. BATHROOM

BECAUSE OF ITS WARMTH AND BRIGHTNESS, YELLOW WAS CHOSEN TO UNIFY THE ARCHITECTURAL ELEMENTS AND FURNISHINGS IN THIS SMALL HOME.

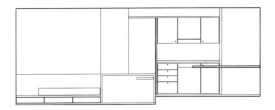

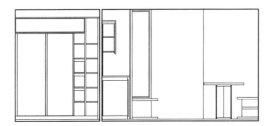

SECTIONS

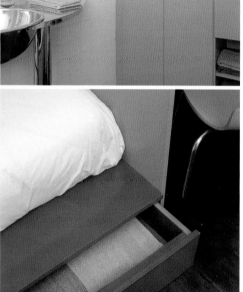

THE BUILT-IN FURNISHINGS, SUCH AS THE KITCHEN
UNIT, CLOSETS, AND THE LONG DINING ROOM BENCH,
HELP MAKE THE BEST USE OF THE SPACE.

ATTIC APARTMENT

ARCHITECT: **RATAPLAN** LOCATION: **VIENNA, AUSTRIA** AREA: **645 SQ. FEET** DATE: **2000**
PHOTOGRAPHY: **MARKUS TOMASELLI**

panes of frosted glass that allow natural light to enter during the day and serve as lamps during the night. They also make it possible to see the space in its entirety, so the bathroom feels less confining. This sensation is reinforced by covering all the interior surfaces with white glass. The use of contrasting colors is the final detail emphasizing the different elements that combine to create this striking interior.

This project called for adding a residence in a small area which for years had been considered wasted space. The apartment is located in a small attic of a hundred-year-old building in downtown Vienna. While the structure made it impossible to have openings on the outer walls, there are several in the roof, flooding the interior with natural light and allowing a feeling of spaciousness.

The first order of business was to take down the old walls that broke up the interior and took up too much space, and replace them with thin metal partitions that serve as a framework for the new elements. Service areas, including the kitchen, bathroom, and bedroom, were placed along the side wall and kept as small as possible in order to maximize the amount of space devoted to the living room. Three elements weave the service areas together: the red kitchen cabinets, which also serve as a dividing wall for the bathroom; a thin wall lined with felt, which was placed alongside the living room and serves as a door to the bathroom; and the wood panel ceiling, which covers the bathroom and part of the kitchen, and forms the bedroom floor.

The placement of the components and the materials and finishes emphasize the idea of lightness, bringing out the specific characteristics of each object. Between the felt-covered wall and the other vertical elements are

RATAPLAN

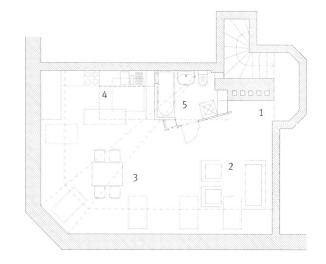

PLAN

1. ENTRANCE
2. LIVING ROOM
3. DINING ROOM
4. KITCHEN
5. BATHROOM

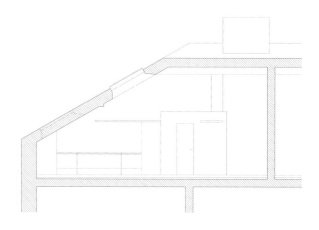

SECTION

THE SET OF COLORED PANELS ON THE LOWER
LEVEL HIDES THE METAL STAIRS LEADING
TO THE BEDROOM, WHICH IS LOCATED ABOVE
THE BATHROOM.

THE NEW ELEMENTS HIGHLIGHT THE ORIGINAL GEOMETRY, CREATING AN INTERIOR LANDSCAPE WITH MULTIPLE PERSPECTIVES, ANGLES, AND SHAPES.

APARTMENT ON OCEAN DRIVE

ARCHITECT: DD ALLEN LOCATION: **MIAMI, UNITED STATES** AREA: **625 SQ. FEET** DATE: **1998**
PHOTOGRAPHY: **PEP ESCODA**

This apartment, on the top floor of an early 1960s building whose style is typical of this part of the city, is used by the owner – who is also the architect responsible for designing the interior – for short stays. Ocean Drive, one of the busiest streets in Miami Beach, is in the midst of a bustling urban center, and the owner enjoys the neighborhood, especially the ine local restaurants. The location, the original character of the space, and the client's needs were the determining factors for the interior design.

To create a sense of spaciousness, the dividing wall, which marked off a bedroom, was removed, leaving a single room. A structural column of reinforced concrete, almost sculptural in shape and form, remains open to view. The kitchen, which doesn't get much use, was reduced to a cooktop with some basic appliances. More emphasis was placed on the bar, next to the built-in refrigerator, ideal for enjoying an aperitif. The bed, fully integrated with the rest of the space, sits on a platform shaped like a grand piano, from which an ocean view can be savored.

Finishes and furniture were chosen with the aim of maintaining the original character of the space. The polished concrete floor is pale turquoise, while the plaster walls are painted lime green. The original 60s and 70s furniture was picked up at small local specialty stores. A minimal number of elements and the color palette combine to create a peaceful, fresh atmosphere in keeping with the city's climate and character.

DD ALLEN

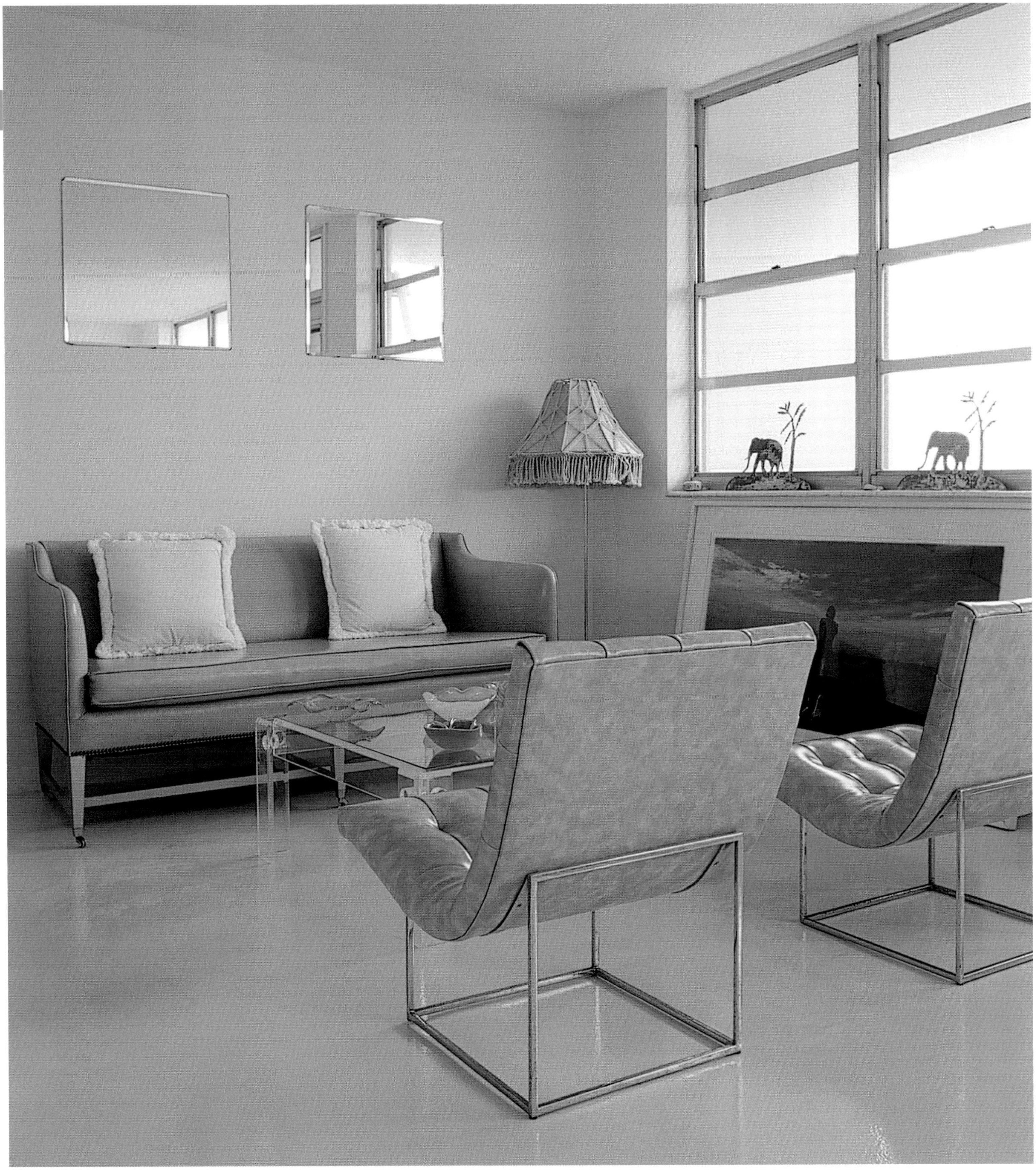

MOST OF THE DESIGN AND DECORATIVE WORK FOR THIS
APARTMENT CONSISTED OF THE SEARCH FOR ELEMENTS
CHARACTERISTIC OF THIS ARCHITECTURAL STYLE.
THE PALE COLOR MAKES A SOFT BACKDROP FOR THE ARRAY
OF OBJECTS FOUND IN LOCAL MIAMI MARKETS.

APARTMENT IN LA BARCELONETA

INTERIOR DESIGNER: **PEPA POCH** LOCATION: **BARCELONA, SPAIN** AREA: **345 SQ. FEET** DATE: **1999**
PHOTOGRAPHY: **STELLA ROTGER**

Although La Barceloneta district, near the port of Barcelona, is an area in which fishermen's homes are traditionally found, this apartment is more reminiscent of a small industrial loft – thanks to the work of the interior designer, who used its architectural features to great advantage.

Originally, the apartment was organized along traditional lines – that is, despite its size, it was broken up into several rooms. The first step in the renovation was to take down the partitions and create a single space in which all activities would take place. Also, the false plasterboard ceiling, which reduced the height of the space and concealed the original structure, was removed. The wooden beams were restored, as were the small vaults between the rafters, increasing height and enhancing the space's unique character. Only the bathroom, where a glass block wall ensures privacy while allowing light to shine through, is completely isolated from the rest of the space. These changes having been made, the apartment was ready for finishing and decorating.

The idea of creating a setting reminiscent of loft space translated into the contrasting use of rustic materials and contemporary furnishings. Old-looking walls and the original wood highlight the modern furniture, gray Formica, and red silestone used in the kitchen and bathroom.

The principal decorative element is the use of color. While small units are often painted white to create the illusion of spaciousness, here colors enhance the qualities of the light and delimit the various areas. Blue reflects the light entering through the windows and is a relaxing color; orange, which stimulates the appetite, was used in the dining area. Finally, a bright pistachio green was used on the only wall that does not receive natural light.

PEPA POCH

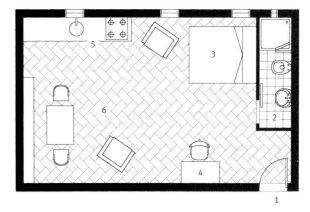

PLAN

1. ENTRANCE
2. BATHROOM
3. BED
4. STUDIO
5. KITCHEN
6. LIVING ROOM/DINING ROOM

ALTHOUGH THE SPACES ARE SMALL,
THE USE OF DIFFERENT COLORS GIVES EACH
AREA ITS OWN SPECIAL CHARACTER.

CREATING A SINGLE SPACE, AND USING
TRANSLUCENT MATERIALS SUCH AS GLASS BLOCKS
TOOK MAXIMUM ADVANTAGE OF THE LIGHT
POURING IN ON ONE SIDE OF THE APARTMENT.

Movable Panels

Spatial flexibility is perhaps the most characteristic feature of any design for a small home. One of the most common ways to achieve that flexibility is to remove the interior walls and partitions, creating not just more space, but space that can be taken advantage of in its entirety for any household function. To avoid opening everything up to view and to ensure some privacy and separate the space into different areas, mobile elements that divide the interior are used. These dividers, which are often light panels that slide on rails and are easily moved from side to side, become objects of great richness in their own right, very important to the overall composition of the apartment.

APARTMENT IN CASA MAGAROLA

INTERIOR DESIGNER: **BÁRBARA SALAS**   ARCHITECT: **JORDI SOLÉ RAFÒLS (BUILDING RENOVATION)**
LOCATION: **BARCELONA, SPAIN**   AREA: **775 SQ. FEET**   DATE: **2000**   PHOTOGRAPHY: **MONTSE GARRIGA**

This apartment was created when a nineteenth century former seminary in Barcelona's old quarter was renovated. Casa Magarola – as the building was originally called – had large balconies, very high ceilings, a carriage entrance, and an extensive central courtyard. The transformation of this building, once devoted to religious purposes, into an apartment complex is part of the strategic plan for the renewal of many formerly depressed areas of the city. Making the most of the original building's fine structural features, the renovation converted it into apartments that are small but of ample proportions, with good lighting and a peaceful ambience.

The interior designer took full advantage of the building's unique features, very similar to those of a typical loft, without adopting the minimalist approach often seen in these types of homes. Thus, she relied heavily on the choice of materials and colors in creating an atmosphere with character. Using the colors of the existing beams as a reference point, she chose iroko wood furniture with contrasting polished stainless steel frames. The bookshelves and stairs, in the same stainless steel, were conceived as superimposed elements, more like furniture than integral parts of the architecture. Two large wooden sliding doors can be used to integrate the kitchen and pantry with the rest of the space or close them off.

Special attention was paid to the selection of colors and the lighting which, in this case, were basic to the desired overall effect. Black was used for the sofas and long drapes, and red for the decorative accents, such as the Moroccan rug, vases, and artwork. The lamps were chosen not just for their design, but also because the brightness of each can be controlled independently, in accordance with the client's needs.

BÁRBARA SALAS

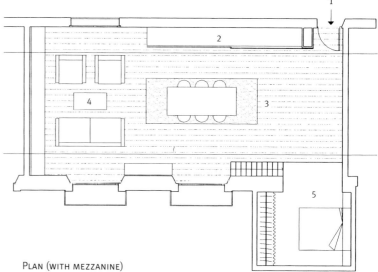

Plan (with mezzanine)

1. Entrance
2. Kitchen
3. Dining room
4. Living room
5. Bedroom
6. bathroom

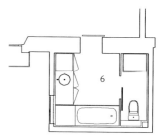

Bathroom plan

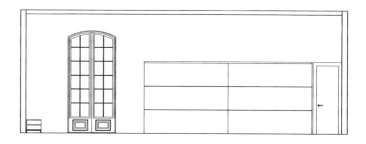

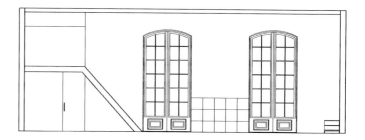

Sections

In addition to allowing the kitchen to be integrated with the rest of the space, the sliding wooden doors are striking elements that blend very well with the character of the existing architecture.

AT ONE END OF THE APARTMENT, THE HIGH-CEILINGS
WERE USED TO ADVANTAGE, WITH THE BATHROOM
BEING PLACED BELOW THE BEDROOM. THE
SHEET METAL USED IN CONSTRUCTING THE LOFT,
A DECORATIVE TOUCH IN AND OF ITSELF, WAS
LEFT OPEN TO VIEW.

MODULAR APARTMENT

ARCHITECT: **GUILHEM ROUSTAN** LOCATION: **PARIS, FRANCE** AREA: **569 SQ. FEET** DATE: **2002**
PHOTOGRAPHY: **ALEJANDRO BAHAMÓN**

This apartment is located in a 30-story building constructed in 1968 by architect A. Zerfus, and its interior responded perfectly to the demands of the era for spatial functionality and natural illumination and ventilation. But the new owners' needs and contemporary requirements provided the impetus for a renovation. The entrance had no natural light, there was insufficient storage space, the living room was very small, especially with respect to the oversized bedroom, and the kitchen was functional but very cramped.

The renovation started with the highly efficient original plan, retaining the advantages of a modern design and taking precise steps to balance the light and space. Long diagonal sightlines were opened up, allowing natural light to pour into the farthest reaches of the apartment. The continuous flooring and the finishes made the rooms seem elongated and less deep, parallel to the façade. Two walls consisting of sliding wooden doors can be arranged in different ways to modularize the kitchen, living room, study, and bedroom spaces. So, though all the rooms are small, each extends into the next, creating a sense of continuity and spaciousness.

The furnishings were kept to a minimum to emphasize the white walls, which reflect the light and provide a background for works of art. Most of the closets are built in, vastly increasing the amount of storage space without filling the apartment with ostentatious furniture. Black slate flooring in the moisture-prone service areas contrasts with the polished wood used throughout the rest of the apartment.

GUILHEM ROUSTAN

THE SLIDING WOODEN DOORS ADD WARMTH
AND MAKE IT POSSIBLE TO COMPLETELY TRANSFORM
THE SPACE, REFERRING BACK TO THE ORIGINAL
PLAN OF THE APARTMENT.

Plan

1. Entrance
2. Bathroom
3. Kitchen
4. Living room/Dining room
5. Studio
6. Bedroom
7. Terrace

THE MATERIALS AND FINISHES ESCHEW ALL DESIGN EXCESS, CREATING A VERY FUNCTIONAL SPACE. THE METAL GUIDES FOR THE SLIDING DOORS ARE VISIBLE AND THE WOODEN SHELVES DOUBLE AS UNOBTRUSIVE ROOM DIVIDERS.

APARTMENT IN MARGARETEN

ARCHITECT: **LICHTBLAU. WAGNER ARCHITEKTEN** LOCATION: **VIENNA, AUSTRIA** AREA: **540 SQ. FEET** DATE: **1997**
PHOTOGRAPHY: **BRUNO KLOMFAR**

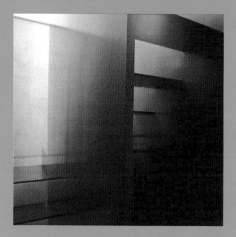

The top floor of a building in Vienna's Margareten district was converted into these four tiny apartments. The architects' goal was to create original, contemporary, functional space without resorting to luxurious finishes and sophisticated details. Rather, the most noteworthy features of this renovation are the low budget with which it

was accomplished and its energy efficiency. Through this project, the architects demonstrate how truly original housing solutions can be achieved. They believe that that the low cost is a direct result of the appropriate melding of the structural, energy, and construction aspects of the project.

The housing units are conceived as two types of symmetrical apartments. An extra area was laid out in between the two apartments and can be annexed to either one. This configuration can easily be accomplished by relocating the dividing partition as desired. To compensate for the small size of the apartments, a common area, placed next to the stairs, is used for storage, as a laundry room, or to expand the social area as needed.

The absence of interior walls and unnecessary finishes resulted in lower costs and is in keeping with the new interior aesthetic. In this case, the finishes are the same polished concrete and glass that also serve as connecting elements. Vertical walls are not needed for the bathroom and kitchen fittings, which are installed under the floor. This strategy,

along with the removable kitchen and bathroom modules, makes it possible to place these two areas anywhere or change their position as desired. This project breaks with the concept of a bathroom independent from the principal space; there are only inconspicuous divisions marked off by sliding doors on slender metal rails.

LICHTBLAU. WAGNER ARCHITEKTEN

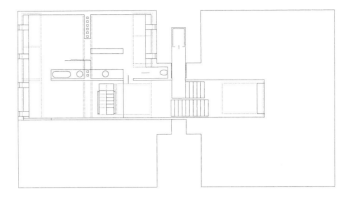

PLAN (APARTMENT 1)

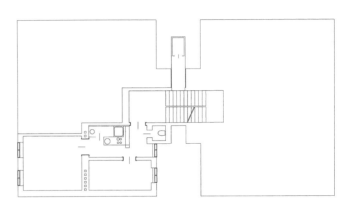

PLAN (APARTMENT 2)

THE STAIRS LEADING UP TO THE SLEEPING LOFT
IN ONE OF THE APARTMENTS BECOME A SCULPTURAL
ELEMENT WITH CONTEMPORARY LINES,
CONTRASTING WITH THE CLASSICAL CHARACTER
OF THE SPACE.

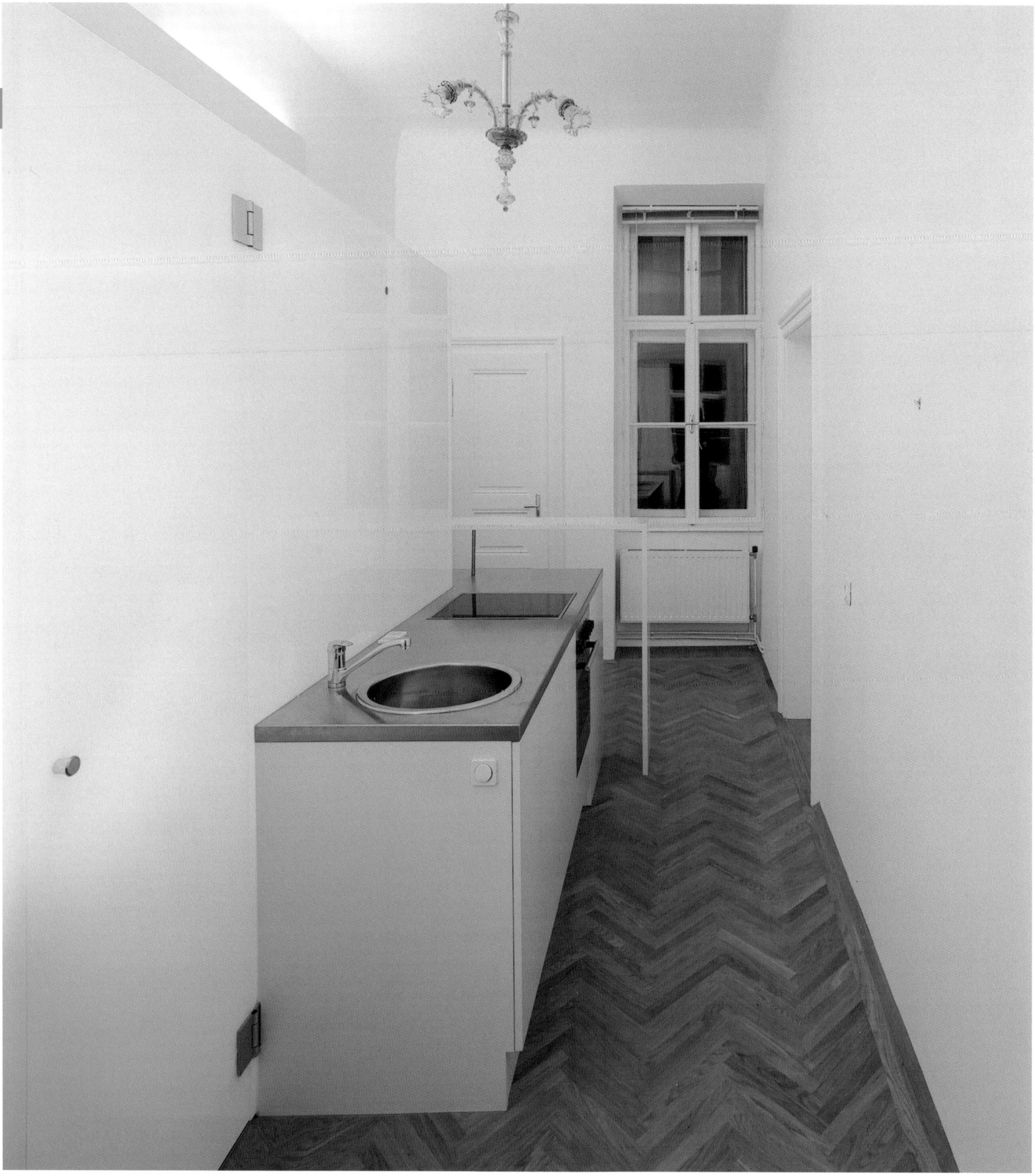

Apartment in L'Hospitalet

DESIGNER: **José Luis López** COLLABORATORS: **Maite Martí, Genaro Rodriguez, Futur-2**
LOCATION: **L'Hospitalet de Llobregat, Barcelona, Spain** AREA: **580 sq. feet** DATE: **1999** PHOTOGRAPHY: **Pep Escoda**

The original tiny apartment had a conventional layout with three bedrooms, a small living room, a kitchen, and a bath. When this layout was eliminated, and the supporting concrete pillars that help to define the new layout were uncovered, the space could be perceived as a whole.

The new plan is an open, continuous space in which all the rooms are integrated through the use of furnishings or the architecture itself. Entry is through a small passageway which also serves as the foyer and leads to the central area, where the living and dining rooms are located. The same passageway also provides access to the kitchen, which is connected with the living room by a hostess bar that also does duty as a dining table. A circular sliding door made of wood and parchment can close the bedroom off from the central space. Only the bathroom is totally isolated.

The materials and finishes play a very important role in achieving contrast between clean lines and warm decorative elements. The bar is faced with glass blocks that support the beech wood top. At night the bar becomes a lamp, thanks to the warm light between the glass blocks and the kitchen cupboard. Beech wood is also used for the kitchen cupboards, the parquet floor, the armoire, and the bed. With a base containing large drawers, the bed also provides storage space. Pórex, which is a material that resembles brick, covers two walls: an interior wall and the wall that backs the façade, providing excellent thermal insulation and soundproofing, and adding a touch of warmth to the interior.

José Luis López

The mix of materials and textures, in the same color family, gives the interior a very rich and welcoming ambience. Beech wood, found throughout the apartment, also covers the rear wall.

Apartment in Gràcia

Architect: **Oleguer Armengol**   Location: **Barcelona, Spain**   Area: **800 sq. feet**   Date: **2000**
Photography: **Stella Rotger**

This apartment was originally the roof terrace of an old building in the Gràcia district of Barcelona. Several years ago, the designer converted it to a shed and for some time it was used as a studio. Then the designer decided to fit it out as a home and make it his personal residence. First the structure was made habitable with thermal and acoustic insulation, and then the interior design work – based on very simple but striking elements – was undertaken and a bright, open apartment was created.

Since the space is regular in shape, it was divided into two distinct areas. Sliding doors divide the interior into a larger space containing the living room, kitchen, and dining room, and a smaller space containing the bedroom, closet, and bathroom. These large sliding doors can open up to integrate the bedroom with the rest of the space. Since they don't reach the ceiling, they do nothing to detract from the feeling of continuity. A well-placed unit separates the living room from the kitchen/dining area. This unit, which also does not touch the ceiling, is a bookcase on the living room side and accommodates two sinks while providing storage and counter space in the kitchen. So the kitchen is, in effect, a central island which doubles as a dining room.

The details, furnishings, and finishings all enhance the feeling of open space and clean lines. The carob wood floor extends to become a raised outdoor deck. To contrast with materials such as steel, natural wood, and gray ceramic, a bright red was chosen for the walls. These tones, combined with the sparse furnishings, make a cozy home in what was once a simple shed on top of a building.

Oleguer Armengol

THE OUTDOOR DECK OFF THE LIVING ROOM OF THIS ROOFTOP APARTMENT EXPANDS THE INTERIOR SPACE, WHILE THE GLASS DOOR PROVIDES ALL THE ROOMS WITH NATURAL LIGHT AND VENTILATION.

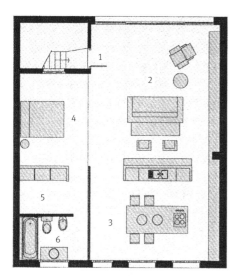

PLAN

1. ENTRANCE
2. LIVING ROOM
3. DINING ROOM/KITCHEN
4. BEDROOM
5. CLOSET
6. BATHROOM

IMPLEMENTS WERE LEFT IN PLAIN VIEW IN BOTH THE
KITCHEN AND BATHROOM, AVOIDING THE NEED TO TAKE
UP A LOT OF SPACE WITH CABINETS AND ALSO CREATING
AN INFORMAL ATMOSPHERE. THE HALOGEN LIGHTING
FROM THE WALL UNIT IN THE KITCHEN IS COMPLEMENTED
BY INDUSTRIAL LAMPS OVER THE DINING TABLE.

RESTRAINT

An effective way to solve any layout problem in a small space is to simplify the design as much as possible. Eliminating the elements that are not essential to the home and creating a setting dominated by clear, pure lines makes the interior seem larger and brighter. Without resorting to minimalism, which involves putting a great deal of time and energy into details and finishes, as well as high costs, restraint in design and décor becomes an effective strategy in these types of projects. The materials used for the interior are generally the same as those used in the building, making for a clearer interpretation of the space, with utilitarian objects of great formal richness providing decorative touches.

Apartment on C. Stahi Street

ARCHITECT: **Westfourth Architecture**   COLLABORATORS: **Vladimir Arsene, Gabriel Bunea, Cristina Stefan**
LOCATION: **Bucharest, Rumania**   AREA: **645 sq. feet**   DATE: **2002**   PHOTOGRAPHY: **Mihail Moldoveanu**

This apartment, located in the old quarter of Bucharest, belongs to an architect who commutes between his offices there and in New York. The building was designed to ensure excellent lighting and ventilation throughout. There are two large windows on the façade, one with a small balcony, and two smaller windows in the rear. These features, and the client's sporadic use of the premises, were the basic determinants of the interior design.

The apartment is arranged around the central corridor, which serves as a reference point for the placement of all the other elements. The entrance is at one end of the corridor, which connects the kitchen and living room while separating the bathroom from the bedroom. A balcony off the living room provides views of the surrounding area, as does the bedroom window, while the service areas were placed close to the small rear windows. While the structure made it impossible to open up the interior entirely, the apartment is nevertheless characterized by continuous, flowing space.

The furnishings and finishes add the defining touch in establishing the apartment's character. Black rubber floor tiles unify all the rooms and require little maintenance. The shelves emphasize the horizontal lines of the space and provide storage areas or work surfaces, and the sliding doors contribute to the sensation of flowing space. Finally, the color white, which helps make the apartment look larger, dominates, not just in the finishes, but also in the furnishings.

Westfourth Architecture

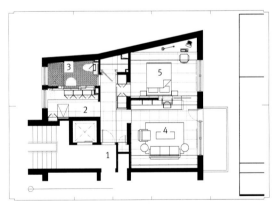

PLAN

1. ENTRANCE
2. KITCHEN
3. BATHROOM
4. LIVING ROOM
5. BEDROOM

INDIRECT LIGHTING, HIDDEN BEHIND THE ARCHITECTURAL
ELEMENTS, EMPHASIZES THE CLEAN LINES AND CREATES
A "GALLERY" EFFECT IN THE LIVING ROOM.

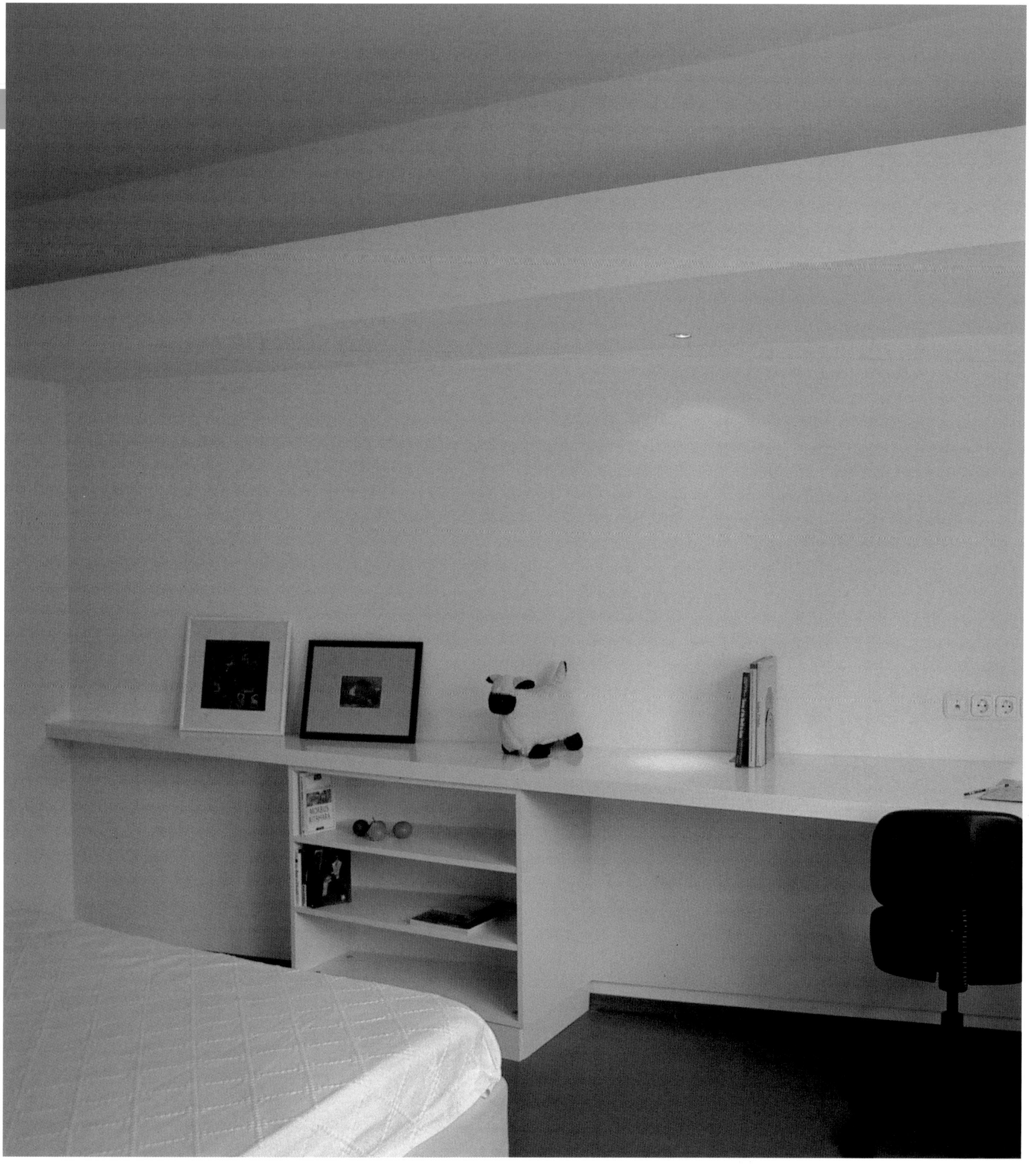

The clean lines and restraint present in the main rooms are also reflected in the kitchen and bathroom. Small openings to the building's central courtyard provide natural lighting and ventilation.

APARTMENT IN SHEPHERD'S BUSH

ARCHITECT: **JEREMY KING** LOCATION: **LONDON, UNITED KINGDOM** AREA: **505 SQ. FEET** DATE: **2000**
PHOTOGRAPHY: **MONTSE GARRIGA**

The plan for renovating this apartment involved creating an efficient home and workspace for one person within the confines of this small area, while providing for the maximum possible amount of storage. A long storage unit was hung on the side wall, leaving free space above and below it, providing a feeling of continuity while respecting the room's original proportions. It holds clothing, shoes, the dryer, housewares and, most importantly, a drawing table and office area. The desk can be folded out of the way when not in use, minimizing clutter in the bedroom.

The second challenge was to design a kitchen with all the modern conveniences, including a dishwasher, washing machine, oven, and refrigerator. The minimal space and the need to create convenient work and storage areas complicated the task even more. Each aspect was studied in great detail, and maximum use was made of every possible surface. Imaginative strategies were employed, such as placing the washing machine in a corner which is normally wasted space in kitchens.

The subtle textures and colors of the materials minimize the impact of the project. Afromosia wood floorboards connect the two spaces and add a warm touch. Bedroom and kitchen furnishings are painted white to blend with the walls. The kitchen worktop, which also serves as a breakfast bar and, extending into the living room, as shelving, is topped with bright lilac Formica, which provides a well-placed touch of color.

JEREMY KING

THE SUBTLE MAKEOVER OF THIS INTERIOR RETAINS
THE ORIGINAL CHARACTER OF THE HOME, USING
WARM MATERIALS SUCH AS WOOD, NATURAL
FABRICS FOR THE CHAIRS AND CURTAINS,
AND A TOUCH OF COLOR IN THE KITCHEN TABLE
AND SOME DECORATIVE ELEMENTS.

■ TWO DOORS IN THE STORAGE UNIT BECOME A WORK TABLE THAT FOLDS AWAY AT NIGHT. THE PURITY OF THE SPACE WAS MAINTAINED BY ANCHORING THE UNIT TO THE WALL WHILE LEAVING OPEN AREAS ABOVE AND BELOW IT.

ROMANTIC APARTMENT

ARCHITECT: **PETER TYBERGHIEN**   INTERIOR DESIGNER: **BRUNO PASCAL**   LOCATION: **PARIS, FRANCE**   AREA: **569 SQ. FEET**
DATE: **1998**   PHOTOGRAPHY: **ALEJANDRO BAHAMÓN**

This apartment is located in Paris's 9th arrondissement, close to Montmartre and minutes from the center of the city. Although small spaces are the rule in large European capitals, this interior has unusual features for an apartment of this type. First, all the areas, including the bathroom and kitchen, have natural lighting and ventilation. Moreover, the unit looks out on a spacious, tree-filled interior courtyard that isolates it from the street, ensuring peace and quiet.

The clients were having trouble finding a comfortable place where they could spend a few days while visiting the city. Tired of trying different hotels, they decided to create their own pied-à-terre that they could also offer to others who wanted to feel as if they had a home away from home.

After studying the clients' needs and the space, the architect knew what he wanted to do. Step one was to open up the space, eliminating the walls that separated the kitchen from the rest of the apartment, creating the sensation of a larger area while making the kitchen a more hospitable place. The bathroom was expanded and the lavatory was placed in an independent space. A double entry provides acoustic insulation between the building's staircase and the living room. The metal beam running across the interior was used to divide the space into two long halves. From it hangs a rail which supports track lights that supply most of the illumination. A long unit on the wall opposite the windows conceals a column that once broke up the space. This

unit now serves as a bookcase, display cabinet, and closet.

A wooden platform placed flush against the end wall adds the finishing touch. It serves as storage space, an extra sofa, and the principal bed. The wooden floor is complemented by soft, warm tones, curtains in natural colors, and austere furnishings, which give the apartment a homey feeling.

PETER TYBERGHIEN

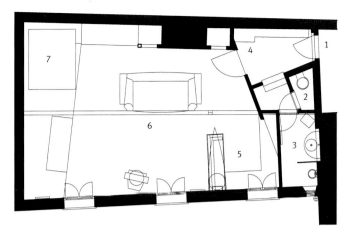

PLAN

1. ENTRANCE
2. TOILET
3. BATHROOM/SHOWER
4. LIBRARY
5. KITCHEN
6. LIVING ROOM
7. BED

THE KITCHEN ALSO FEATURES A VIEW OF THE INTERIOR COURTYARD THROUGH A WINDOW
BY THE SINK. A WOODEN BAR SERVES AS A DINING TABLE AND CONNECTS THE KITCHEN
WITH THE LIVING ROOM.

THE WARM MATERIALS, SUCH AS WOOD AND NATURAL FIBERS, CONTRAST WITH THE AUSTERE LINES AND DECORATIVE OBJECTS TO CREATE A COMFORTABLE, PEACEFUL ATMOSPHERE.

APARTMENT IN DORNBIRN

ARCHITECT: **GELI SALZMANN**   COLLABORATOR: **EDITH GRABHER (ART)**   LOCATION: **DORNBIRN, AUSTRIA**   AREA: **440 SQ. FEET**
DATE: **1998**   PHOTOGRAPHY: **IGNACIO MARTÍNEZ**

Originally, the house in which this apartment is located was a tavern and blacksmith's stable in a small, idyllic plaza in Dornbirn, Austria. In 1998, as part of a project designed by architects Christian Maier, Philip Lutz, and Geli Salzmann, the tavern was renovated and the stable was converted to a studio and apartment. This general strategy served as the starting point for the transformation of the space into a tiny home.

The apartment is situated in the upper part of the structure, just below the building's sloping roof, which gives the interior space its pronounced triangular shape. While this unconventional shape makes the usable area rather small, it also creates a feeling of spaciousness. To retain that feeling, the floor plan was kept undivided and open. The service areas, including the lavatory, shower, and storage facilities, are separated by units that stop short of the ceiling.

The interior design highlights the interaction between the visible parts of the building's original structure and the finely finished surfaces and furnishings. Wood chipboard panels, plasterboard, stucco, and marble finishes are combined. The wooden furnishings consist of pieces designed to perform multiple functions. The cooktop is also the dining table and the sideboard is the rear part of the bathroom.

With a touch of playful whimsy, Austrian artist Edith Grabher, taking the crucifixes traditionally found in a corner of the living room as her point of reference, has placed golden antlers on a surface painted to look like the sky.

GELI SALZMANN

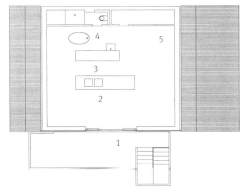

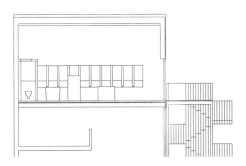

Plan

1. Entrance
2. Dining room
3. Kitchen
4. Bathroom
5. Bed

Longitudinal section

Transversal section

THE RENOVATION RETAINED SOME OF THE ORIGINAL
COMPONENTS, SUCH AS THE WOODEN BEAMS,
WHICH WERE EXPOSED WHEN A SKYLIGHT
WAS ADDED.

The space is organized around two units of furniture laid out parallel to the entrance: the large table that serves as the dining area and cooktop, and the sideboard that marks off the bathroom. The unique character of the space is achieved by combining contemporary pieces with more rustic objects and materials.

Apartment in Lisbon

ARCHITECT: **Inês Lobo** COLLABORATOR: **Rita Zina** LOCATION: **Lisbon, Portugal** AREA: **590 sq. feet** DATE: **2000**
PHOTOGRAPHY: **Sergio Mah**

This apartment in a narrow building in the heart of Lisbon faces both the street and the interior courtyard. Thus, it has good natural light and ventilation, and the thoughtful placement of the original walls was the basis for the new layout. This is an elongated space with the entrance in the center, emphasizing the division of the apartment into two distinct areas.

The striking design, blending beautifully with the existing architecture, is based on simple, restrained lines. The living room is on the street side; the dining room, kitchen, and bathroom are on the courtyard side; and the two darker, quieter central spaces were reserved for the closet and bedroom. One continuous storage and shelving unit skirts the side of the apartment and the walls perpendicular to it like a second skin covering the interior. This unit clearly divides the space into four rooms that accommodate the various living functions. Used as shelving, bookcases, storage compartment, and a combined kitchen shelf/counter facility, it defines and links the rooms.

White dominates throughout, on the walls and ceilings as well as the continuous unit. Thus, all the unit's functions are merged and integrated with the architecture, providing a neutral background which highlights everyday objects such as books, pieces of furniture, and household appliances. The natural pine floor, which contrasts with the white surfaces, covers the entire apartment, adding a warm touch.

Inês Lobo

The color white, present in the architectural components and the ubiquitous wall unit, is a unifying element that helps link one room to another.

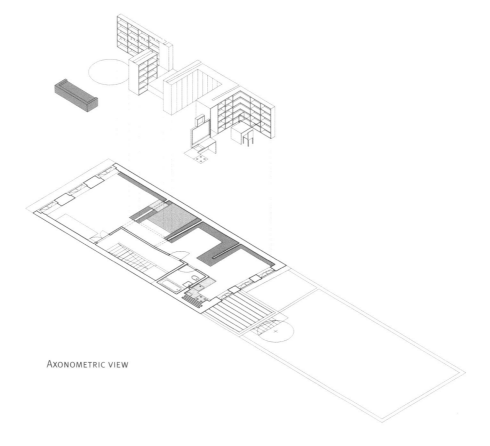

AXONOMETRIC VIEW

EXTERIOR

A feeling of spaciousness in an apartment is largely a function of the relationship established with the outdoors. In addition to seeking optimal natural light and ventilation throughout, the design of these apartments makes the outdoors an integral part of the home. In some cases, the property itself has a balcony, garden, or courtyard that is connected to the interior spaces of the apartment through large windows or sliding glass doors. While it's not always possible to include an outdoor area as part of the home, large windows, panoramic vistas of the city, or views of an interior garden add depth to the interior.

BOLLARINO APARTMENT

ARCHITECT: **UdA / Walter Camagna, Massimiliano Camoletto, Andrea Marcante** LOCATION: **Turin, Italy**
AREA: **785 sq. feet** DATE: **2001** PHOTOGRAPHY: **Emilio Conti**

This apartment was created as a result of the restoration of an old home in the heart of Turin, Italy. What was once a cramped three rooms has become an ample space for a small home of pleasing proportions. The building retained its original structure of brick walls with few openings on the sides, and boasts a glass-enclosed balcony overlooking a peaceful, tree-filled interior courtyard. Making the most of this old structure, the project creates a contemporary interior language that contrasts with the character of the building and its surroundings.

The principal challenge was to link the glassed-enclosed balcony, with its view of the garden, to the rest of the existing space. To accomplish this, the dividers that previously broke up the space were almost entirely eliminated. Only the structural walls were retained, and these served as a point of departure for marking off the various areas. The original three rooms were replaced by a generous, continuous space. The bathroom with shower takes on a great formal richness that blends with the existing wall, the glass skylight, the painted metal beams, and the glass sliding doors. This area becomes the focal point that defines the living and dining areas as well as the kitchen, creating an interesting play of transparencies, light, and color. The bedroom, closet, and bathroom were placed in the rear of the apartment, where there is less light and more peace and quiet.

The permeability of the space and the play of reflections produced by the glass are also visible from the outside. Red metal beams create a certain dynamism that interacts with the structural walls.

UdA / WALTER CAMAGNA
MASSIMILIANO CAMOLETTO
ANDREA MARCANTE

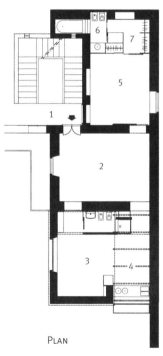

PLAN

1. ENTRANCE
2. LIVING ROOM
3. DINING ROOM
4. KITCHEN
5. BEDROOM
6. BATHROOM
7. CLOSET

Opening up the interior space made it possible to enjoy views of the garden from almost anywhere in the apartment. This, along with the height of the ceilings, creates a feeling of spaciousness.

The details and finishes stand out because of their simplicity. A set of three sliding doors in the bedroom makes the entrance to the bathroom and closet a subtle composition.

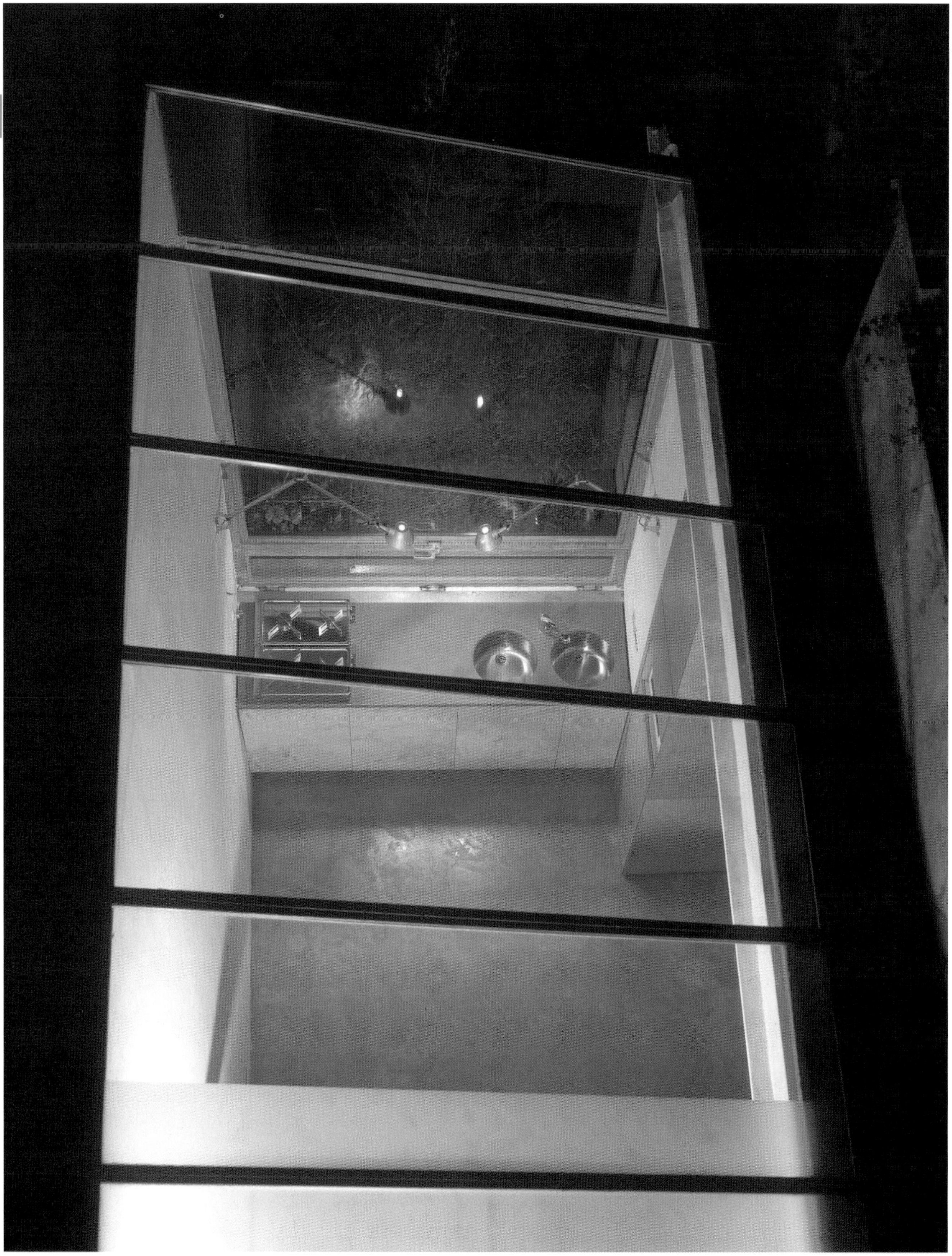

APARTMENT IN BRUSSELS

INTERIOR DESIGNER: **CATHERINE DE VIL**   LOCATION: **BRUSSELS, BELGIUM**   AREA: **731 SQ. FEET**   DATE: **2000**
PHOTOGRAPHY: **STELLA ROTGER**

This home is situated in a 1970s building in central Brussels, surrounded by a peaceful landscaped area. The apartment has a terrace that provides natural light and ventilation while extending the interior. Despite the building's prime location, the space lacked a specific character of its own – very common in many buildings of that era. The main objective of the interior design was to give the apartment the character of a place that has been lived in for quite a long time.

The strategy was to choose a small number of elements that would create an atmosphere midway between rustic and minimalist. Integrating the tiny kitchen with the living and dining area was one of the priorities. This resulted in both spaces seeming larger and was more in keeping with the occupants' lifestyle. The flooring was replaced with untreated fir floorboards, which require less maintenance and impart a feeling of age and rusticity. The flooring integrated all the areas of the home, including the terrace, where the same flooring was used.

The other decorative elements are along the same lines, creating an overall effect that is restrained and homogeneous. Cotton and linen in natural colors are used for the sofa coverings and curtains, which are hung from wrought iron rods. The colors, also in a range of natural tones, create a peaceful atmosphere with little contrast. Only the kitchen, in gray and blue, stands out a little from the rest of the space, although here, too, the overall effect is one of simplicity. The furnishings and cupboards hide most of the appliances, while an iron frame hanging from the ceiling holds some accessories.

CATHERINE DE VIL

Although the apartment is located in the heart of the city, the terrace, the materials, and the decorative touches combine to create a rustic atmosphere.

APARTMENT IN JANELAS VERDES

ARCHITECT: **JOÃO MARIA VENTURA** COLLABORATOR: **NUNO PINTO** LOCATION: **LISBON, PORTUGAL** AREA: **322 SQ. FEET**
DATE: **2001** PHOTOGRAPHY: **SERGIO MAH**

The building containing this apartment is located in Lisbon's old quarter, very close to the Tagus River. Population growth over the centuries has resulted in high density in this part of the central city, which has, in turn, left behind housing types that are difficult for modern urban dwellers to accept. This apartment looks out on neither the front nor the rear of the building; it has only an interior courtyard to provide the light and ventilation necessary for a home.

The objective of this low-budget project was to turn this two-story space into a comfortable home for a single person. On the upper level, which contains the entrance, space was freed up as much as possible to create a long, narrow living room. At one end, an opening to the courtyard offers a view of the tree that grows there. On one side of this level the bathroomand kitchen are located, with a small dining niche near the window. The lower floor houses the bedroom, defined by a bed surrounded by four walls, the laundry room, placed under the stairs, and the exit to the courtyard.

The impact of the limited floor space and low height minimized by the light that filters through the tree's leaves. Painting all the walls white made the best of these less-than-ideal conditions. The neutral surface and the northern light create an ideal backdrop for the contemporary paintings the client has collected through her work as a gallery owner.

JOÃO MARIA VENTURA

FIRST FLOOR

GROUND FLOOR

LONGITUDINAL SECTION

TRANSVERSAL SECTION

1. ENTRANCE
2. BATHROOM
3. KITCHEN
4. DINING ROOM
5. LIVING ROOM
6. BEDROOM
7. COURTYARD

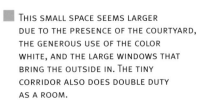

THIS SMALL SPACE SEEMS LARGER DUE TO THE PRESENCE OF THE COURTYARD, THE GENEROUS USE OF THE COLOR WHITE, AND THE LARGE WINDOWS THAT BRING THE OUTSIDE IN. THE TINY CORRIDOR ALSO DOES DOUBLE DUTY AS A ROOM.

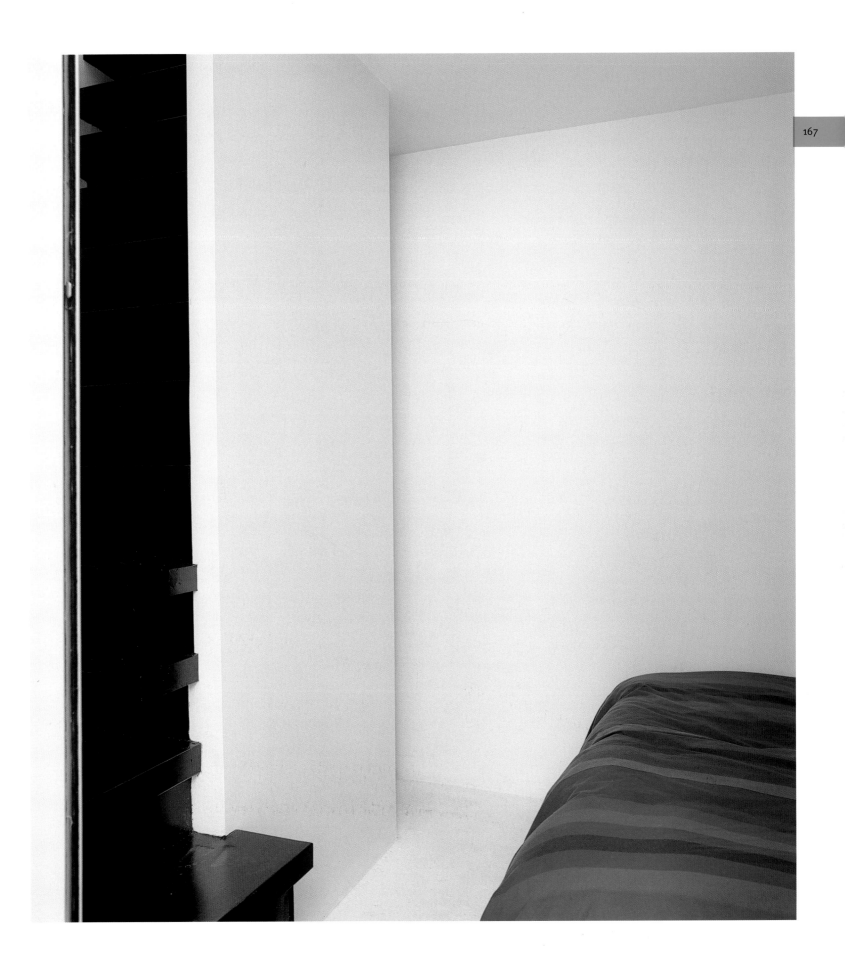

Photographer's apartment

Architect: **Tanner Leddy Maytum Stacy Architects** Location: **San Francisco, United States**
Area: **755 sq. feet** Date: **1997** Photography: **Stan Musilek, Sharon Reisdorph**

This photographer's apartment is an expansion of an existing industrial structure located on San Francisco's Potrero Hill. The owner had previously converted this former paint factory into his own photography studio. Later on, he decided he wanted to have the option of living there, in order to enjoy the advantages of its structure and location, but in a space separate from the work area. The original building consisted of a basic rectangular unit with structural walls of concrete block and a roof built on a framework of wooden beams. The new home, superimposed on the original structure, enjoys splendid views of the city and the bay.

The apartment is laid out as part of a series of spaces, one after the other. The studio is located on the ground floor, followed by a mezzanine and the upper floor, where the living space is located, with the roof serving as an outdoor terrace. Thus, the spaces become brighter and more open as one ascends from the closed, dark photography studio.

The mezzanine serves as a connecting space between the work and living areas. It is here that the kitchen, bathroom, and storage areas are found. Since the original building already had a large kitchen and bathroom, the renovation only slightly supplemented them. This service area is separated by a staircase from the main living space, which contains the bedroom, dining room, and living room. Here a panoramic view of the city dominates the interior. Unlike the service area, this space contains no divisions except a sliding glass door that partitions off the bedroom. Huge windows integrate the balcony and the view with the home's interior.

Tanner Leddy Maytum Stacy Architects

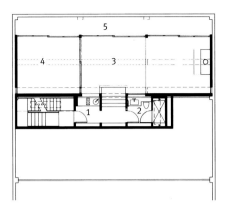

PLAN   1. ENTRANCE/KITCHEN
        2. BATHROOM
        3. LIVING ROOM/DINING ROOM
        4. BEDROOM
        5. TERRACE

■ THE NARROW EXTERIOR BALCONY AND LARGE
WINDOWS MAKE FOR FABULOUS PANORAMIC
VIEWS OF THE CITY AND SAN FRANCISCO BAY.

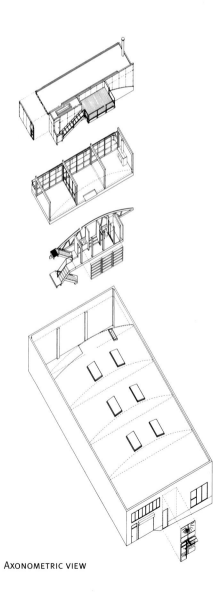

AXONOMETRIC VIEW

THE KITCHEN AND THE BATHROOM ARE ON
A LEVEL SLIGHTLY BELOW THE MAIN SPACE,
BUT THEY ARE VISUALLY CONNECTED TO
THE HIGHER LEVEL.

Apartment
on Flinders Lane
Staughton Architects

1st floor 59 Hardware Street
Melbourne 3000, Australia
T. +61 3 9642 4820
F. +61 3 9642 4810
starch@bigpond.com

La Magdalena
Apartment
Guillermo Arias

Ctra. 11 Nº 84-42 Int. 5
Bogotá, Colombia
T. +57 1 257 9501
garias@telefonica.net.co

West Village Apartment
Desai / Chia Studio

54 West 21st Street 7th floor
New York NY 10010
United States
T. +1 212 366 9630
F. +1 212 366 9278
kchia@desaichia.com

Apartment
on Michigan Avenue/
Bishop's Manisions
Apartment
Pablo Uribe

411 Fulham Palace Road
London SW6 6SX, United Kingdom
T. +44 20 7731 1420
pablouribeuk@hotmail.com

Apartment on
Rue Rochechouart/
Romantic Apartment
Peter Tyberghien

Begijnhoflaan 45
9000 Gent, Belgium
T. +32 92 23 69 36
F. +32 22 53 113
peter@tyberghien.be
www.tyberghien.be

Apartment
on Baró de la Barre
**Araceli Manzano
Mª José Manzano
Esther Flavia**

Ausiàs March 31, Pral. 2ª
Barcelona 08010, Spain
T. +34 93 302 4688

Attic Apartment
Rataplan

Kohlgasse 11/3
Vienna, 1050 Austria
T. + F. +43 1 544 0625
rataplan@eunet.at

Apartment
on Ocean Drive
DD Allen

80 Eighth Avenue #1602
New York, NY 10011
United States
T. +1 212 627 5440
F. +1 212 727 1930
info@pierceallen.com

Apartment
in La Barceloneta
Pepa Poch

T. +34 639 505 696

Apartment
in Casa Magarola
Bárbara Salas

Goya 14, 1º-2ª
Barcelona 08012, Spain
T. +34 617 89 6771
F. +34 93 307 1833
barbarasalasbcn@hotmail.com

Modular Apartment
Guilhem Roustan

22, Rue de la Folie Méricourt
75011 Paris, France
T. +33 1 43 55 80 04
F. +33 1 40 21 69 14
guilhem.roustan@free.fr

Apartment
in Margareten
LICHTBLAU. WAGNER ARCHITEKTEN

Diehlgasse 50/1718
Vienna, 1050 Austria
T. +43 1 54 518 54-0
F. +43 1 54 518 54-4
office@lichtblauwagner.com

Apartment in L'Hospitalet
JOSÉ LUIS LÓPEZ

Roc Bonorat 37
Barcelona 08005 Spain
T. +34 93 485 3100
F. +34 93 486 4049
info@futur-2.com
www.futur-2.com

Apartment in Gràcia
OLEGUER ARMENGOL

Bonavista 22, bajos interior
Barcelona 08012, Spain
T. +34 93 217 5986
F. +34 93 237 7804
estudio22@terra.es

Apartment
on C. Stahi Street
WESTFOURTH ARCHITECTURE

627 Broadway, Suite 504
New York, NY 10012
United States
T. +1 212 388 9227
F. +1 212 388 9228

Apartment in
Sheperd's Bush
JEREMY KING

27 Maldon Road
London W3 6SU, United Kingdom
diggie.king@btinternet.com

Sheperd's Bush in Dornbirn
GELI SALZMANN

Mühlebacherstrasse 25
Dornbirn 6850, Austria
T. +43 5572 29827
F. +43 5572 29827 21
geli.salzmann@aon.at

Apartment in Lisbon
INÊS LOBO

ilobo@mail.telepac.pt

Bollarino Apartment
UdA / WALTER CAMAGNA
MASSIMILIANO CAMOLETTO
ANDREA MARCANTE

Via Valprato 68
Turin 10155, Italy
T. +39 011 2489489
F. +39 011 2487591
uda@uda.it
www.uda.it

Apartment in Brussels
CATHERINE DE VIL

T. +33 1 46 24 96 16

Apartment in Janelas Verdes
JOÂO MARIA VENTURA

24 de Julho, 90, 2º dto
1200 870 Lisbon, Portugal
T. + F. +351 21 395 4566
jmtrinidade@mail.pt

Photographer's Apartment
TANNER LEDDY MAYTUM
STACY ARCHITECTS

444 Spear Street #201
San Francisco CA 94105
United States
T. +1 415 495 1700
F. +1 415 495 1717
www.lmsarch.com